The First

teddy bears

Pictures and Price Guidelines

By Peggy and Alan Bialosky

Published and Distributed by:
Alan and Peggy Bialosky
% Ontario Printers, Inc.
1150 West Third Street
Cleveland, Ohio 44113

Printed in the United States of America

Acknowledgments

The authors gratefully and warmly thank and acknowledge the special people who helped with the research and preparation of this book. With deep appreciation, their most sincere gratitude goes to:

B. F. Michtom,

Hans-Otto Steiff,

and

Shirley Bertrand, "Shirley's Dollhouse"; Edson J. Brown and Ross Trump, "Brown-Trump Farm"; Stephen A. Butler, R. Dakin & Company, Richard Frantz, Ed Freska, Pat Garthoeffner, "Toy Box Antiques"; William D. Gearhart, H2W, Inc.; Susan Heller, John Hoffa, Ideal Toy Corporation, George R.Jenskovic, Ruth Kalb, Morton Kane, Roland M. Kraus, Robert Ciancibello and James Pappas, "Pappabello Antiques"; Jan Pitney; Don and Mary Jane Poley, "Mary Jane's Dolls"; Reeves International, Inc.; William Russ, Klee Sherwood, Joan Silberbach, Margarete Steiff GmbH, Richard Steinfirst, Taggart's Toys and Hobbies; Rose Vargo, and The White Elephant Sale of Cleveland, Ohio.

Photographs by Peggy and Alan Bialosky and Stephen Butler. Cover design by Ed Freska.

Dedicated to David, Jeff and Randy
who have had to learn to live with Bears.

Foreword

"TEDDY BEARS: Pictures and Price guidelines" has been compiled by utilizing our own experience, and by comparing the additional opinions of collectors, dealers and authorities over a geographically distributed area. The purpose of this book is to give readers a general idea as to the value of Teddy Bears. This is not a final authority. It is to be used only as a suggested guideline.

Teddy Bears have become extremely collectible, and prices are rising. Values listed here are based on the market at the time this book is published. (Prices will vary, depending upon a Teddy Bear's size, condition, appeal, quality, etc.) We will update this book in future editions in the years ahead.

While every effort has been made to be accurate, the writers and publishers are neither liable nor responsible in any way for any errors in prices, information, identification or typography.

In addition, every effort has been made to provide appealing enough photographs to make this book a pleasure for any bear fancier of any age to own.

We sincerely hope you and your bears will enjoy this volume as much as we enjoyed compiling it.

Thank you very much for buying it.

Introduction

In 1902, while on a hunting trip, President Theodore Roosevelt refused to shoot a captured bear. This act was immortalized a short time later when it was depicted in a political cartoon by Clifford Berryman in the Washington Post. It received a great deal of attention.

Aware of this, Morris Michtom, a Brooklyn, New York shopkeeper displayed two toy bears in the window of his stationery and novelty store. His wife, Rose, had made them: light colored plush, stuffed with excelsior, and complete with shoe button eyes. Michtom sought and received permission from the President himself to call the new toys "Teddy's Bears".

The Michtoms' plush bears became an appealing success, as well as the foundation of the company we know today as The Ideal Toy Corporation.

In addition, the Steiff company in Germany, known for its unusually fine quality stuffed animals, also reports having made a toy stuffed bear during this historic 1902-1903 period. The Steiff bear was exhibited at the Leipzig Fair in Germany in 1903, and is reported to have been shown the following year in St. Louis, Missouri, at the St. Louis World's Fair.

For both companies, Teddy Bears became an important item throughout the years to follow. These toys also became an important part of family life.

Many of the old Teddy Bears survived, and are still treasured as companions or as ornaments. They are kept, not only by children, but by adults of all ages as well. Today they are also prized by many serious collectors.

Why not? After all, the Teddy Bear is no mere toy; it is a symbol of warmth and security in an everchanging world.

Who would ever turn down such a friendship?

A rare treasure: an original Ideal Teddy Bear,
made in 1903. One of these is in the
Smithsonian. Note the fine quality, and the shoe
button eyes.

Photo by permission of The Ideal Toy Corporation.

Margarete Steiff pictured with one of her Teddy
Bears; 1980 will mark the Steiff Company's
100th anniversary. The organization is planning
to produce a 17 inch Teddy Bear which will be
available in the United States, possibly in
March, and will be limited in edition. A
tremendous demand will probably make this an
extremely popular item.

Photo through the courtesy of Margarete Steiff, GmbH.

Christopher Robin's famous and popular
original toys, including the illustrious
Winnie-the-Pooh. They make their home with
E. P. Dutton and Company in New York.

Photo by permission of E. P. Dutton and Company.

Odds and Ends . . .

Old Teddy Bears rarely had reliable identification on them, such as antique dolls had. During the years of research that preceded this book, the authors personally interviewed almost a thousand Teddy Bears.

The ones selected to appear in the photographs on these pages, were selected for their quality, appeal, personalities and/or authenticity. (If any readers would care to send us photographs and information pertaining to their own bears, we would be pleased to have them for our files.)

During research, several problems appeared:

Teddy Bears, who were loved alot for a great many years, lost not only their hair, but occasionally their size. A Teddy originally measuring 17 inches, for instance, may have been squashed to a shorter height, or lengthened to the point where it could play center on a basketball team.

Also — Steiff buttons appeared, as bears became collectible, glued on to bears that were not manufactured by that company. Along these lines, a few bears made in Poland in the 1970's appeared at increasing numbers of antique shows and flea markets with their labels removed, and their fur artificially aged. Their prices also had quickly changed: from the original two or three dollars they sold for, to $25 dollars or more. Let buyers beware. If one is not sure of a Teddy, and the price is substantial, it is wise not to buy it.

Eyes were another variable. Old bears who originally saw the world through shoe buttons, sometimes had transplants: glass eyes with metal loops or stick pin backs, etc. These were the result of normal childhood experiences, and the values of Teddy Bears shouldn't be lessened by ophthalmic mishaps.

Paw pads also had to be replaced. Bears are, after all, animals with plantigrade habits: they walk on their soles with their heels touching the ground. So, of course, they often wear out the felt. If left unrepaired, some Teddies develop the sloppy habit of leaking stuffing. Therefore, replacements sometimes become urgent necessities. These should be done with minute stitches and old fabric of the proper type and color. When correctly done, paw replacements should not greatly alter the value of a bear.

Squeakers, growlers, and musical mechanisms also may have been removed, replaced, or put out of commission through the years. In some cases, clothing was added; it was usually from the same period as the Teddy wearing it.

Teddy Bears were stuffed with any of a variety of materials: straw (stiff and crackly, if you feel it), excelsior (softer, more like sawdust), kapok (for a softer, huggable quality), and wood-wool (for a firmer piece). Wood-wool was a type of wood fiber that was processed to resemble wool. Kapok was used for stuffing mattresses and came from the seed pods of certain trees sometimes referred to as silk-cotton trees. Some bears were stuffed with a combination of these materials.

Mouths, noses, and paw embroidery was sometimes done with coarse mercerised cotton thread.

The covering of early bears was usually mohair. This was fabric made from the hair of Angora goats, but the term also applies to fabric made of a wool and cotton blend. Mohair can have either a stiff or soft feel to the touch.

Plush was a fabric with nap longer than that found on velvet. It included silk, cotton and wool combinations. Plush has a softer feel to it. The scent of old straw-and-mohair in authentic old Teddy Bears is a familiar and identifying one to the advanced, experienced collector.

Some old Teddy Bears are extremely soiled. The quickest way to clean one is to vacuum the toy gently to remove loose dust and debris. (Always check for signs of moths or silverfish if the bear has been stored in an attic or basement.) Then, using a long-handled soft bristle brush lightly apply a mild, diluted liquid soap solution. Brush on gently with overlapping circular motions. Afterwards, rinse off with a clean brush dampened with clear water to which a small amount of good quality fabric softener has been added. (This helps remove mats from clumped fur.)

Dry lightly with a bath towel. Then dry with a hair dryer while combing with a good metal (dog grooming) comb to raise the pile and separate it as it dries. A small fine tooth metal comb called a "flea" comb works especially well.

Keep in mind: it is always a risk to clean an old bear.

Never store Teddy Bears next to a heat register or a radiator. Closed glass door bookcases or cabinets are ideal for display purposes.

The nicest part about collecting Teddy Bears is that it's a fun thing to do. Among the old hand-made ones, no two are alike; you are acquiring a sort of soft sculpture piece of art — something which, properly cared for, will still be loved by generations to come.

Happy bear hunting!

A Guide to the "Guidelines"

About the Authors

Peggy and Alan Bialosky have written a pet column for The Plain Dealer in Cleveland, Ohio, for more than 12 years. In addition to being interested in animals of all kinds, they have a special fondness for Teddy Bears. They have studied and interviewed them for almost 20 years. The Bialoskys have written other books, as well as magazine articles, and most of the pictures in this book are the result of their other hobby: photography. Some of their own bears appear above, and will vouch for their character and kindness to bears.

18½ inches, gold mohair, bell in stomach,
hump, glass stick pin eyes, jointed at hips and
shoulders, swivel head, straw stuffed. $125

17½ inches, early 1900's, cotton fabric, original
clothes, shoe button eyes, straw stuffed.
Unusual. $110

13 inches, early 1900's, soft brown mohair,
squeaker, glass eyes, jointed at hips and
shoulders, hump, swivel head, felt paws, black
sewn nose and mouth, straw stuffed, nose
elongated from forehead, wideset ears. Very
nice unusual expression. $165 up

20 inches, brown mohair, squeaker, glass eyes, jointed at hips and shoulders, swivel head, felt paws, black sewn nose and mouth, straw stuffed. Exceptional quality. $250 up

(Book pictured: "Der faule Teddybar", color plates, inscription dated 1928, German. $55)

15 inches, gold mohair, hump, squeaker, shoe
button eyes, jointed at hips and shoulders,
swivel head, chubby body and limbs, black
sewn nose and mouth, very wide set ears,
hard-soled feet, straw and
kapok stuffed. $150 up

15 inches, Steiff, early 1900's, white mohair,
shoe button eyes, humps, jointed hips and
shoulders, swivel heads with softer stuffed
stomachs, squeakers, felt paws, light brown
sewn noses, mouths. Rare pair. $200 each, but
more if you can find a matched set.

19 inches, gold mohair, glass eyes, jointed at hips and shoulders, elongated torso, swivel head, original felt paws replaced, black sewn nose and mouth, stiffly stuffed with straw. $95

13 inches, Steiff type, early 1900's, shoe button
eyes, gold mohair, growler, hump, jointed at
hips and shoulders, swivel head, felt paws,
black sewn nose and mouth, straw stuffed, worn
spots on body. $125 up

19 inches, gold mohair, squeaker, shoe button
eyes, hump, jointed at hips and shoulders,
swivel head with heart-shaped face — unusual
expression, felt paws, black sewn nose and
mouth, straw stuffed. $120-$130

16 inches, light gold mohair, squeaker, shoe
button eyes, hump, jointed at hips and
shoulders, elongated torso, short legs, swivel
head, felt paws, black sewn nose and mouth,
wood-wool stuffed. $150

23 inches, light gold mohair, replaced paw felt,
glass stick pin eyes, hump, jointed at hips and
shoulders, swivel head, fabric nose, brown
sewn mouth. Body and limbs are plump and
stiff to the touch; straw stuffed. $150

20 inches, Steiff, light mohair, 1920's, squeaker, glass eyes, jointed at hips and shoulders, swivel head, felt paws, brown sewn nose and mouth, straw stuffed. $150-$185

Oak child's rocker, cane seat. $55

8 inches, mohair, squeaker, glass eyes, hump,
jointed at hips and shoulders, swivel head with
long nose, felt paws, brown sewn nose. Stands
or sits and looks like miniature Grizzly. Very
appealing. $110

12 inches, Steiff, gold mohair, squeaker, glass
eyes, jointed at hips and shoulders, swivel
head, felt paws, brown sewn nose and mouth,
straw stuffed. $110

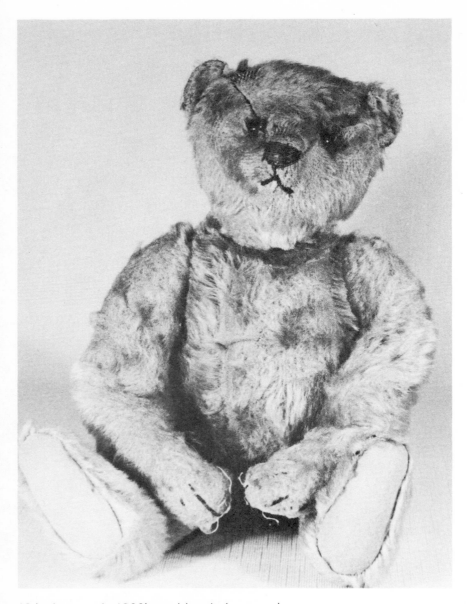

13 inches, early 1900's, gold mohair, squeaker, shoe button eyes, hump, jointed at hips and shoulders, swivel head with small ears, felt paws, black sewn nose and mouth, straw and excelsior stuffed. $165 up

15 inches, gold mohair, 1910-1920, close set
shoe button eyes, squeaker, hump, jointed at
hips and shoulders, swivel head, felt paws,
black sewn nose and mouth,
straw stuffed. $150

13 inches, brown mohair, squeaker, glass eyes,
small hump, jointed at hips and shoulders,
brown sewn nose and mouth, swivel head, felt
paws, straw stuffed. Very appealing. $100 up

24 inches, gold mohair, glass stick pin eyes, jointed at hips and shoulders, swivel head, replaced felt paws, black sewn nose and mouth, very chubby torso, straw stuffed but very firm to the touch. $165

13 inches, light brown mohair, squeaker, glass
eyes, small hump, jointed hips and shoulders,
swivel head, felt paws, straw stuffed. $100 up

21 inches, 1930's, gold mohair, glass stick pin eyes, pear-shaped torso, jointed at hips and shoulders, swivel head, felt paws, brown sewn nose and mouth, straw stuffed. $100 up

20 inches, gold mohair, circa 1915-1920,
squeaker, glass stick pin eyes, jointed at hips
and shoulders, swivel head, felt paws,
straw stuffed. $115

Pink and white high button leather boots with
pink pearl buttons and pink silk tassels, $8

13½ inches, circa 1920, German, gold mohair, glass stick pin eyes, squeaker, unusual facial expression, jointed at hips and shoulders, swivel head, felt paws, black sewn nose and mouth, straw stuffed. Note wide set ears. $165

14 inches, 1930's, glass eyes, squeaker, red felt
paws, hump, jointed at hips and shoulders,
swivel head, elongated stiff body with short
arms, black sewn nose and pouty mouth,
straw stuffed. $65

15 inches, Steiff "Koala", mohair, squeaker,
jointed at hips and shoulders, legs are bent in
curved position; felt nose and open mouth,
swivel head, bendable fingers and toes. Unique
appearance. $150

17 inches, Steiff, button in ear, 1920's, gold
mohair, glass eyes, jointed at hips and
shoulders, swivel head, felt paws, brown sewn
nose and mouth, straw stuffed. $175 up

13 inches, Steiff, early 1900's, gold mohair,
squeaker in body, shoe button eyes, hump on
back, jointed at hips and shoulders, swivel
head, felt paws, black sewn nose and mouth,
straw stuffed. $165 up

25 inches, gold mohair, squeaker, glass eyes,
jointed at hips and shoulders, swivel head, felt
paws, black sewn nose and mouth, elongated
torso, short arms, thin legs, stiff,
hard body. $150

18 inches, gold mohair, squeaker, glass eyes,
large head with upturned nose, thin limbs
jointed at hips and shoulders, swivel head, felt
paws, straw stuffed. $110 up

13 inches, Steiff, brown mohair, not original but old collar with tag engraved "Teddy", jointed at hips and shoulders, straw stuffed. $165 up

13 inches, early 1900's, gold mohair, shoe button eyes, jointed at hips and shoulders, swivel head, felt paws, black sewn nose and mouth, excelsior stuffed. $100

13½ inches, gold mohair, squeaker, glass eyes,
black sewn nose and mouth, jointed at hips and
shoulders, felt paws, swivel head, thin limbs,
straw stuffed — very hard to the touch. $100

19 inches, brown mohair, glass eyes, jointed at
hips and shoulders, swivel head. $100-$135

15 inches, 1930's, gold mohair, glass stick pin
eyes, hump, jointed at hips and shoulders,
swivel head, thin torso and limbs, black sewn
nose and mouth, straw stuffed. $125

13 inches, Steiff, glass eyes, hump, jointed at
hips and shoulders, swivel head, felt paws,
black sewn nose and mouth,
straw stuffed. $150

15 inches, white mohair, glass stick pin eyes,
hump, jointed at hips and shoulders, swivel
head, linen paws, light brown sewn nose and
mouth, straw stuffed, thin limbs. $100

20 inches, Steiff, white mohair, deep low-voiced
squeaker, glass eyes, jointed at hips and
shoulders, swivel head, felt paws, brown nose
and mouth. Extremely lovable. $200 up

19 inches, light gold long mohair, early 1900's, hump, glass stick pin eyes, jointed at hips and shoulders, swivel head, felt paws, brown sewn nose and mouth, straw stuffed. Grizzly bear appearance. Unusually appealing. $200 up

22 inches, gold mohair, growler, shoe button
eyes, modified hump, jointed at shoulders and
hips, swivel head, felt paws, black sewn nose
and mouth, straw stuffed. $135-$150

21 inches, cinnamon mohair, squeaker, shoe
button eyes, jointed at hips and shoulders, large
swivel head, plump torso and limbs, brown
sewn nose and mouth,
straw stuffed. $135-$150

12 inches, Steiff, early 1900's, mohair,
squeakers, shoe button eyes, humps, jointed at
hips and shoulders, swivel heads, felt paws,
straw stuffed. $165 up/each

7 inches, gold mohair, squeaker, hump, shoe
button eyes, jointed at hips and shoulders,
swivel head with long upturned nose, elongated
torso and thin limbs, black sewn nose and
mouth, straw stuffed. Unusual $85-$100

9 inches, Steiff button in ear, gold mohair, 1907,
shoe button eyes, squeaker, hump, jointed at
hips and shoulders, swivel head, felt paws,
black sewn nose and mouth, straw stuffed.
Finest quality and condition. $150

21 inches, Steiff, gold mohair, growler, glass eyes, hump, jointed at hips and shoulders, swivel head, felt paws, black sewn nose and mouth, straw stuffed. Finest quality. $150 up

22 inches, "Roddy", made in England, glass
eyes, very unusual because it is a puppet type:
move the tail and the head moves up and down
or from side to side, felt paws, jointed at hips
and shoulders. $250

14 inches high, light gold mohair, glass eyes,
muff with quilted lining. Rare. $200-$250

9 inches, old Steiff, button in ear, gold mohair,
glass eyes, original clown hat and ruffled collar,
jointed at hips and shoulders, swivel head,
hump, black sewn nose and mouth,
straw stuffed. $175

16 inches, soft doll type, bright colored stitched-on clothing, brown poodle-cloth type head and paws, satin-like foot pads and ear linings, soft stuffed. $10

Wind-up plush bear on metal scooter, probably German. $55 in working condition

12 inches, gold mohair, early 1900's (skates were added in the 1930's), squeaker, glass stick pin eyes, hump, jointed at hips and shoulders, swivel head, felt paws, black sewn nose and mouth, straw stuffed. $125

15 inches, white long mohair, glass eyes, music box in torso activated by squeezing, jointed at hips and shoulders, swivel head, felt paws. Circa 1930's. Unusual. $175

8 inches high, tin jack-in-the-box type of Teddy
Bear with parasol. Wood handle turns and
music plays while bear bobs up and down.
Rare. $150

23 inches, red, white and blue, about 1918-19, called an "electric eye bear" because eyes are bulbs, battery is in torso. When stomach was pressed, eyes would light up. Jointed at shoulders, straw stuffed. Unusual. In working condition: $200

3¾ inches, early 1900's, mohair, black button type eyes, jointed at hips and shoulders. Head is removed to show glass perfume bottle.
Rare. $65

Lithographed tin tea set with early Teddies on
tray, cups, pot, etc. $85

1970's, plastic Teddy Bear doll size dishes,
made in Germany. $6

6 inches, Steiff, brown mohair, glass eyes,
jointed at hips and shoulders, original ribbons,
swivel heads, brown sewn noses and mouths,
straw stuffed. $65 each

Wooden maple bed, $15

19 inches, mohair head and paws, white cloth
covered sack-type torso and limbs, glass eyes,
original black-yellow cotton suit, swivel head,
black sewn thin nose and mouth, straw and
cork stuffed. Sometimes referred to as a "Teddy
Bear doll". $100

Collection of assorted small bears in a wood
wagon from the early 1900's. Note wood wheels
and hand-painted word "Teddy". Wagon — $75

26½ inches high, German, wood dollhouse made as a tree trunk, hinged and containing three floors. Furniture and bears pictured are not original. $250 for house; substantially more if all original furniture and bears are intact. This was originally carried by F.A.O. Schwarz in New York, discontinued about 7 years ago.

3½ inches, Steiff, mohair, shoe button eyes,
jointed at hips and shoulders, swivel head,
black sewn nose and mouth. $85

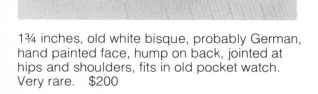

1¾ inches, old white bisque, probably German,
hand painted face, hump on back, jointed at
hips and shoulders, fits in old pocket watch.
Very rare. $200

15 inches, orange plush, orange paws, round,
flatter type face, growler sounds like "Mama"
doll, jointed at hips and shoulders,
straw stuffed. $25

15 inches and 12 inches, Steiff, rare pair of "dancing bears", circa 1910. Glass eyes, jointed at hips and shoulders, swivel heads, dressed in blue jacket (left) and blue plaid pants, blue skirt (right) with violet bodice. Bears are attached at paws and shoulders. $750.

8 inches high, Steiff, button on ear, mohair, has tail and squeaker, metal wheels, swivel head. $125

9 inches high, dark brown mohair, 1930's, black collar, glass stick pin eyes, hump, tail, felt paws, straw stuffed. $55

20 inches (including wheels), Steiff, brown
mohair, hump, glass eyes, brown sewn nose,
growler operated by pulling heavy wire in back,
straw stuffed. $250 in working condition.

19 inches, made in U.S.A., white mohair, glass
stick pin eyes, squeaker, jointed at hips and
shoulders, swivel head, felt paws, black sewn
nose and mouth, soft stuffed. $150

5 inches, made in Japan, gold plush-like bear in
"hat box", jointed limbs, glass eyes, black metal
nose. $15

4½ inches, plush bendable bear with wood high chair (slide out tray on swivel). $10 for both

20 inches, dark brown long pile, tag on stomach
reads "Knickerbocker Toy Company Inc.",
velvet paws, jointed at hips and shoulders,
swivel head with rounded face, black sewn
nose and mouth. $75

13 inches, gold plush, black button eyes, round
head with long nose, jointed at hips and
shoulders, swivel head, velvet paws, black
sewn nose and mouth. $20

24 inches, white mohair, squeaker, glass eyes,
jointed at hips and shoulders, swivel head, felt
paws, black sewn nose, soft stuffed. $150

36 inches, light gold mohair, Steiff, growler
mechanism operated by wire pulled from back,
hump, glass eyes, jointed at hips and
shoulders, swivel head, felt paws and open
mouth, label reads "U.S.-Zone
Germany". $1,200

6 inches, brown and cream wool type plush,
black button eyes, black sewn nose and mouth,
made in England, soft stuffed, Koala-sort of
appearance. $10

8 inches and 10 inches, 1960's, gold or dark
brown mohair, glass type eyes, squeakers, felt
paws, jointed at hips and shoulders, swivel
heads. Small, $35; large, $50

12 inches, "Merrythought", made in England,
tag on right foot. Wide set ears, light brown
plush, jointed at hips and shoulders, swivel
head, unusual face, very well made. $55

15 inches, Chad Valley, 1950's, made in
England (original tags on foot and stomach),
gold mohair, jointed at hips and shoulders,
swivel head, brown felt paws, black sewn nose
and mouth, soft stuffed. $65 up

6 inches, brown mohair, cream paws and
muzzle, original skirt and bow, "Mutzli" on tag,
made in Switzerland. Bear is bendable, and
also will stand. Black sewn nose and
mouth. $20

6 inches, mohair, Steiff, 1953, original ribbon
around neck, squeaker, jointed at hips and
shoulders, swivel head, felt paws, brown sewn
nose and mouth. $95-$125

Miniature wood duck pull-toy, made in
Germany, hand painted. $15

12 inches, 1930's, gold mohair, glass eyes,
jointed at hips and shoulders, swivel head,
pouty face, straw stuffed. $110

17 inches, Steiff, older "Zotty", brown-
and-cream shaded fur, growler, jointed at hips
and shoulders, swivel head, felt paws, brown
sewn nose, open felt mouth. $100

21 inches, 1930's, light mohair, glass eyes,
wearing handmade Teddy Bear bib; jointed at
hips and shoulders, swivel head, felt paws,
soft stuffed. $85

21 inches, cinnamon mohair, squeaker, black
glass stick pin eyes, modified hump, jointed at
hips and shoulders, swivel head, velvet paws,
black sewn nose and mouth, soft stuffed. $85

13 inches, 1950's or 60's, fat felt
"Winnie-the-Pooh" with original red shirt and
black button eyes, black felt nose, stitched-on
arms and legs. $25

6½ inches, circa 1930's, brown felt
Winnie-the-Pooh with 4 inch pink felt Piglet, both
jointed at hips and shoulders, glass eyes,
delicately sewn noses and mouths. $65/pair

18 inches, dark brown plush, hump, jointed at
hips and shoulders, swivel head, velvet ear
linings, velvet paws and muzzle; pudgy torso
and limbs. $30

13 inches, dark brown plush, solidly stuffed, sits
or stands, jointed at hips and shoulders, long
nose, high set ears, felt paws, black sewn nose
and mouth. $25

15 inches, yellow-gold mohair, "Character",
black button type eyes, jointed at hips and
shoulders, swivel head with rounded face and
muzzle, felt paws, plump torso and limbs. $20

10 inches, 1940's, brown plush, black
button-type eyes, "Character" label,
soft stuffed. $25

17 inches, brown plush with cream paws,
squeaker in tail, plastic eyes, "Ideal" on label,
molded nose and mouth, soft stuffed. $40

16 inches, "Smokey the Bear", Ideal Toy Corporation. Yellow
plastic hat, "Smokey" on belt, ranger badge on chest, talking
mechanism. In 1953, Ideal was given permission to make and
sell Smokey Bear dolls; the company also printed Junior Forest
Ranger cards and packed one with each doll. Some 16,000
youngsters applied to be Junior Forest Rangers on these cards,
and Ideal was honored with a "Golden Smokey" award in 1967
for its contribution.

Smokey doll in working condition: $60.

7 inches and 11 inches, made in Poland and
sold in the 1970's. Tan or dark brown, jointed at
hips and shoulders, soft stuffed. $5 or less for
small one; $10 or less for large one.

12 inches, 1970's, plush, squeaker, unusual
eyes reminiscent of Googlies, tag reads:
"original Heinhauser, made in Germany", black
sewn nose, painted mouth, jointed at hips and
shoulders, stationary head. $15

18 inches including hat, "Paddington", Eden
Toys Inc., 1970's, brown with darker feet, blue
coat and yellow hat. Available in other outfits.
Very well made and very popular. This size:
about $16

16 inches, 1978 Ideal Collector's edition, brown
plush with lighter muzzle and paws, excellent
quality, 75th anniversary special edition
box. $11-$15

24 inches, "UFB" (Unidentified Flying Bear),
made in U.S.A., tags say "Possum Trot" and
designed by Gillian Bradshaw-Smith. Bear
wears space suit, pack straps to back,
removable helmet. $26

7 inches, tag reads: "Misha — Official Mascot of 1980 Moscow Olympic Games." Label includes "Image Factory Sports Inc. R. Dakin & Company." This size sells for about $8, but larger sizes are available.

20 inches, 1970's Peggy Nisbet, made in
England, original autographed tag and label
from "Collector's Edition", jointed at hips and
shoulders, swivel head, black sewn nose and
mouth. $85

17 inches, Basic Brown (B.B. Bear) Bear, made
by H2W, Inc., brown plush, plastic eyes, floppy
limbs, black felt nose, black sewn mouth, soft
stuffed. About $26, clothes (variety available)
extra.

15 inches, Steiff, 1970's, platinum-mink colored (left) luxurious fur texture and appearance, tag: "Minky Zotty", growler, brown sewn nose, felt mouth. (Right) 15 inches, Steiff, white with brown, "Cosy Teddy", brown nose, felt mouth. $100 up/each

Sampler

Teddy Bear related items also are collectible:

Books: "Teddies", Samuel Gabriel Sons & Company, linenette, color pages $15

"Teddy-B & Teddy-G The Bear Detectives, by Seymour Eaton $55

"The Traveling Bears in Outdoor Sports" by Seymour Eaton $30

China: German, old, two white Teddy Bears in open green pocketbook $55

Mug, 1920's, hand painted three bears (Roosevelt Bear style) with surrounding holly design $12

Cup: For a baby, silver plated with early Teddy Bears in relief. Dated 1907 . . . .$40

Doll Blanket: Cotton flannel with early Teddy Bear on either side $25

Fortune-Telling Teddy Bear: The J. M. Bour Co., Royal Garden Tea . . . .$10 with original paper envelope.

Jewelry: 14k gold Teddy Bear with movable jointed limbs and hump on back, on gold chain $175

Knife: Pocket, Roosevelt Bears cut out and in relief on either side. Marked Morgan Import Company, but made in Germany $85

Pin cushion: Marked "The Avery Stamping Co." $10

Postcards: Roosevelt Bears $10 and up, depending upon condition, etc.

Pottery, Buffalo: 6 inch bowl with Roosevelt Bears . . . .$125. (This type of item is extremely collectible.)

Print: Jessie Wilcox Smith from Collier's magazine. Three Teddy Bears with kneeling child $35

Rubber: Candy mold, old fashioned Teddy Bears, 3¾ inches high $10

Teddy Bear: Perfume holder, 1970's, with "jewels" in bow on neck. Hinged to conceal perfume. $15